Wakefield Press

Nearly Lunch

Tall when necessary, **Peter Bakowski** has been writing poetry for 38 years. He remains influenced by the following quote, attributed to Robert Frost—"Make your next poem different from your last." In 2015 Éditions Bruno Doucey of Paris, published a bilingual selection of his poetry, titled *Le coeur à trois heures du matin*. Later this decade Éditions Bruno Doucey will publish a further bilingual selected, titled *La saison du courage*. In Australia in 2022 Recent Work Press will publish his next solo poetry collection, titled *Human News*.

A curiously haunted figure, yet 'serene' for all that, **Ken Bolton** lives in Adelaide where for a long time he ran the Experimental Art Foundation's Dark Horsey bookshop and the Lee Marvin readings. Recent collections include *Starting at Basheer's* (Vagabond) and 2020's *Salute* (from Puncher & Wattmann). Shearsman (UK) issued his *Selected Poems* in 2013, replacing an earlier *Selected Poems* published by Penguin.

Also available from Wakefield Press, the authors' *Elsewhere Variations*, companion volume to *Nearly Lunch*.

Nearly Lunch

Peter Bakowski and Ken Bolton

Wakefield
Press

Wakefield Press
16 Rose Street
Mile End
South Australia 5031
www.wakefieldpress.com.au

First published 2021

Front cover image—*High Noon, Ortigia*, Fran Daddo
Back cover image—*Laneway, Osaka*, John Levy
Typeset by Michael Deves, Wakefield Press
Printed by Finsbury Green, Adelaide SA

ISBN 978 1 74305 859 6

A catalogue record for this
book is available from the
National Library of Australia

Wakefield Press thanks
Coriole Vineyards for
continued support

"Lunch-time, nearly!

Is it? It feels like lunch."

—Martha Hyer

Contents

SIXPACK FIVE

SIXPACK SIX

SIXPACK SEVEN

SIXPACK EIGHT

SIXPACK NINE

SIXPACK TEN

ENVOI

Acknowledgements

Some of these poems, or earlier versions of them, have appeared in the *Canberra Times, Shearsman* (UK) and *Social Alternatives*.

Grateful acknowledgement is made to the editors.

SIXPACK ONE

Phone Call

"You've picked up at last." "What, so you've been ringing?"

"Sure—*just for the last few days.* How are you feeling?"

"Like I'm not really here. I've only been awake

in stages. But apparently I'm going to be fine. And you?"

"Well, I'm sick of *this* place. It's a rest, but I'm bored.

I only sleep in fits and starts, over." "'Over'?

Filipe, you're not on the car radio now." "Habit.

McFerran was in yesterday, by the way. Said he'd

'called by'—but you were 'sedate'." "Well, I probably was. I was *under sedation.*

What'd he say?" "Nothing about us." "No questions then?

He's bound to start. Part of the job." "My daughter Isabelle

does it, you know. Told her grandfather—when he asked her

why she wasn't talking—that she was waiting for him

to say 'over'—otherwise she wouldn't know when to begin."

"What are you talking about, Perez?" "The phone. She copies me

on the phone." "Okay, got it. Call you back in a few minutes.

The nurse is here. Over." "Ha ha."

Nurse Cumel hands over ward duties to Nurse Bradley, New York-Presbyterian Lower Manhattan Hospital

I reckon the guy in Bed 4 is a cop. I can smell cop—
they're always profiling Puerto Ricans
believe we all like spicy food, live to dance.
Hell, my whole walking life I've had grief with corns and bunions—
all those shifts waiting tables to pay my way through nursing college.

That foot grief is still with me. My podiatrist, he's a looker,
Greek, around 35. Beautiful hands. Some nights when Freddie's
snoring beside me I imagine those hands going north, south,
slewing to the left and right on the soft edges of my body.

Well, a woman has a right to fantasize. It beats emptying bedpans.
Anyway, the cop in Bed 4 is on a morphine drip. I reckon the precinct
he's patrolling right now is Cloud 9. I guess he's a cop.
Remember that with him it's still nil by mouth and keep those
restraining straps secured.

Nurse Cumel walks to the staff canteen with Nurse Bradley

New guy in Bed 12, Doris.
Animal Management Officer—
fancy moniker for a dog catcher.
Very sloppy eater—
globs of oatmeal all over the sheets,
even on his bedside phone.
Stares at the ceiling, when he's not
pressing his bedside buzzer.
Man, he sure can fill a bedpan.

Some sort of accent,
possibly South American.
He's looking mighty pale—
well, he nearly got to high five
the guy upstairs.

Rabies. Causes inflammation of the brain.
I'm more of a cat person.
I know they've got a reputation
for being aloof
but my Tabitha
will rub up against any leg—
I was a bit like that in high school,
had boy fever.

Sometimes I have to slap myself—

Freddie and I have been married for 40 years.

Sure, he's got a belly on him now and

most weekends you'll find him on the golf course,

but in the evenings on the sofa

when we're watching *Seinfeld* re-runs,

he'll sometimes pat me on the knee.

Considering Views

The ladder, Paul? says Jane, and I say
it's only two storeys and this saves a lot of time,
and she nods. The mobile scaffolds have to be manhandled
round the flower beds and take a while to unload. As she knows.
She badly hurt her hand a few weeks back. Is it still
bandaged? It was until Friday.   She watches.

On these big windows, when they're really clean
(the reflected sky, and cloud and planes, vapour trails—*anything*)
it looks spectacular and ideal. And *silent*—

the action

is so far off.

And traffic noises, construction, the contractor's lawnmower—
don't seem to impinge. I won't fall off, I tell my supervisor,
and she says, as I know she will, *It's the insurance.*
It won't cover you with just the ladder. I'll be careful, I say
which is enough to allow her to light a cigarette, make
a phone call or whatever. "Okay," I say, when I'm down—
"Jane?"—and she drags the trolley with the tarp and cleaning products,
and I carry the ladder.

Honey

"Honey, how are you?" "I'm fine I think. I *feel* fine.

I'd rather be home." "Would I be able to look after you?"

"Sure, sure. They look at me once, twice a day—*and tell me to

rest*." "Well you should. Look, I brought you these, and this."

"This is Bella's work?" "Frankie helped. He made the bit on top, see?

Whoops, it's fallen off. Still, you get the picture: *they love you*."

"Ah, wonderful kids. Tell 'em not to worry." "I saw Frank on the

way in. He was sleeping—didn't say anything. But his wife was there.

I introduced myself. She's very nice. You might meet her.

She said she'd call on you, to say hullo. Said Frank spoke

highly of you. Curious to meet you." "I spoke to him yesterday.

He was going to call back, but I haven't heard."

"Well, 'Helen'—(is that what you said?)—says she still hasn't

spoken to him herself. So you're way ahead." Filipe's wife unpacks clothes—

T-shirts mostly—some paperbacks, and finally some grapes. "He'll ring

when he wakes up. Helen said you'd be in the same ward soon, she thought."

"I'm moving?" "He's coming here."

Victor Flaxmann, heart surgeon

After a day of operating
I go for a swim in the bay.

The first dive
is a release.

I cherish
the chill, the repetition of wave after wave
and that last year no one died
under my watch.

I keep up with the literature,
borrow heart op videos
from the medical library
but I know
one day
a patient will fade
beneath my guided hands,
despite the years of experience,
despite data and monitors.

Perhaps that event
will shelve me and I'll retire.
Perhaps I'll turn again to books of theology.

I swim and swim
until I'm more
tired of body
than troubled
by my thoughts.

SIXPACK TWO

Portrait of Claude Hartigan

Sunday mornings
I sit in the backyard on the old sofa
which Jacinta found in the street.

It's a good share house.
I get along well with Cedric,
Jacinta's cousin.
We've connected via music,
are both into obscure disco,
especially out of Philly.

It's a quiet neighbourhood,
lots of young families.
Last year Jacinta had a miscarriage,
but we're trying again.
Jacinta's quit smoking,
doctor's orders.

Since my car accident,
all the rehab sessions,
getting strength back in both arms—
I've been working up the courage
to paint again.

Out here on the sofa,

I hold out my painting hand.

It's steady. I can turn my wrist without wincing.

I'll start with a self-portrait,

now that I'm six months sober.

Engagé?

"*That's* an old song you're singing," the voice
from over the fence, of Janey the neighbour. I don't know
her really. I see her out and about, a little, at weekends
coming or going. Minds her own business—we put the bins
out sometimes at the same time. "What was I singing? Oh,

'Directly'." I can't see her but I can see
the clothes on her line are in motion, the clothes hoist rotating:
we are both hanging out washing—or taking it in
in my case. "My brother played it," she says, "and another thing
you sing a lot—about a Cadillac." "I'm guessing

an older brother, right? I stay resolutely
behind the times." She laughs. I can't place the song.
"A Cadillac?" "You sing it a lot," she says. "So I sound—

a *lot*—

like a moron?" I ask. And she says No. (What *could* she say? What
else could she *think*?) "It had 'Communism' in it!" Gone.

I hear her screen door close behind her and her offered clue.
Communism—does that redeem me, or make me
some other kind of nut? I suppose it depends:
if she's a Republican then I've been ticked off. Her clothes
would suggest otherwise—Baader Meinhoff, Red Brigade—she

13

drives a truck, and, like it, looks determinedly functional

most of the time. I don't drive, I ride a bike. Non-functional.

'Scraping by' … 'non-functional'—what *is* my look?

What should I be humming—Joni Mitchell, Saint Etienne? *Brook*

Benton?? 'Ninety-Nine Luft Balloons'? 'Short People'?—

that might put her on her mettle.

Martin, Martin

"Who gave us these?"

"A woman from the Scout Hall," says Martin.

"Well," says Betty, despairing.

She had meant the question rhetorically. "God knows

what they were thinking," she says, eyeing the books again:

Modern

Business English; *The Life of the Spider*; *Mark, the Match Boy*;

Fables in Slang; *Dave Dawson of the Air Corps*; *Penrod Jasper*;

The Wit and Wisdom of Good Pope John; *Boy Ranchers in the Desert*;

A Mother's Prayer; *Best Loved Poems of the American People*; *The Curse*

of Darwin; *Tom Sawyer*; *Crystal Vision* (two copies); *The Ordeal*

of Harriet Marwood, Governess; *Letters For All Occasions*; *A Heap o'*

Livin'; *A Pocket History of England*; *Ginger Meggs*; *Sergeant Silk,*

the Prairie Scout; *Adventures of Ulysses*; *The Southern Oscillation*

Index; *Gold Fools*

—all in a box, wooden, with metal handles

on either side. Would once have had a lid.

"We could give them to the hospital," she says. "They sometimes

come down here asking for books." And "*What?*" she says to Martin—

who says, almost *sotto voce,* "Will they thank us?"—picking up the books

and taking them down the road. Not a lot of fun, Martin. Not

a lot of fun those books. Did the scouts *read* that stuff?

Decisions

The twin brothers, Darren and Albert,
died within nine weeks of each other.

I bought their garage
from the surviving sister, Moira,
who's lived in Noosa since 1969,
prefers yachts to cars.

Floorboards, a skylight and a cooking range installed,
I've named the studio, *Paint Job.*

The split with Jacinta. That was hellish.
I realised that the demands of a child, of becoming a father,
would diminish my painting hours—
I'd be called upon to be a less selfish man.

I've found a doctor here
who'll perform a vasectomy.
A very clean clinic.

Nadine Flagg, day manager,
the Suds-A-Lot Laundrette

With my microfibre cloth I make sure
that the glass front of each tumble dryer is clean.
People like to view their washing,
hear the clack clack of shirt and trouser buttons
against the rotating barrel.

In my apron pockets
I've got one and two dollar coins
to make change.
Most regulars
bring their own laundry powder—
it works out cheaper
and many of them have switched
to eco-friendly brands.

The radio was my idea—
brighten up the place.
Oldies station. They play a lot of sixties soul—
Aretha, Otis, The Supremes. Choice Atlantic and Motown.

Little Johnny seems to like the music.
Cosy in the portable bassinet,
sometimes he wiggles his toes.

Mr Peterson has been kind to me,
letting me bring Johnny to work.
His mother was a single mother too.
There are some good men in this world.

I'm taking a break from relationships,
learning about solitude.
Give me a 5000 piece jigsaw puzzle
and I can forget the world for a while.

Front loader number four is out of order.
The repairman will be here soon.
Tall Sudanese guy. Handsome. The whitest teeth.

Hospital Stores

Woss-this-shit!? says Margaret bitterly—

amused and cocky, pleased to see Martin.

Martin wonders if Margaret is drunk already.

But she spins about confidently and puts things aside,

making room for the box, picks a book out

for a brief examination

and laughs. "Who reads this stuff?"

"My view entirely," says Martin, "Quiz nite tonight?"

he ventures, "—down at the *Four-Leaf*?" "Yeah, see you there, 6.30

maybe—for dinner first up." "Right. *Be* there."

"Oy?" "*I'll* be there. See you." Martin exits.

Margaret wheels on her good leg—her 'better' leg—

to peer after him—as he leaves the loading bay, out into

the daylight—her lips pursed as she calibrates

whatever it is—his mood, his height, his shirt.

Martin sometimes catches her watching him ("as if

shrewdly"—he has said to himself. Shrewd about what?)

The promise of the night is cheering, Margaret's touchiness though

taking off a little of the shine. But she likes his humour.

Back to Betty.

SIXPACK THREE

Shifts

"Nurse? How often are you monitoring this patient?"

"Every half hour—the same as Nurse Cumel was doing."

"And she reported no change, no fluctuations?" "No,

she said all the readings had been steady."

Doctor Prescott—who was young like herself

and seemed good at his job—kind enough, thorough—

usually called Emma by her name. Over the week

he may have forgotten. But no! "Emma—

Nurse Stanley, isn't it?—if you could keep a close eye on her …

When does your shift end?"

"10.30." "Keep an eye on her—half-hourly will do—

and let me know if things change, even just a little."

"I will." "I'm here till 6.30." He smiled.

"She's going to be okay," he continued. "Yesterday it didn't

seem so certain." "Old," said Emma, regarding the patient,

"Eighty-three." "Yes, but strong enough it looks like.

We'll get her up and moving—gardening, isn't that what she talks about?"

"She used to be on TV when I was a child, I think." "Really?"

"Yes, I thought she was old then." "There you go.

Well, she's going to get older." He smiled and turned,

and turned again as he walked away—"if

there's any change." "Yes, Doctor."

Elsa Mertens, cleaner

This is my thirty-fifth year of service.
The things I've found in staff wastepaper baskets—
empty flasks of brandy and gin,
used condoms, especially in the photocopier room,
and one time, three crumpled attempts at a suicide note.

But hospital morale has improved
since Mr Henson made CEO.
Free staff fitness classes,
more vegetarian and vegan choices on the canteen menu
and monthly outings to wildlife sanctuaries
in a courtesy bus.

At the annual fundraiser in Claymore Gardens,
he's there, wearing a joke apron,
manning the barbeque,
selling raffle tickets,
driving the hired ghost train.

His personal assistant, Tiffany,
told me that he's been known
to work ninety hours.
Little wonder his wife filed for divorced.

Sometimes I see him standing dead still
in a corridor, momentarily lost.

I keep him in my Sunday prayers.
He must never become a patient.

Doris Bradley, senior nurse

After a shift,
if the weather's OK,
I take a stroll through Claymore Gardens.

You'll get the occasional tour group,
there to take photos of each other
standing by the statue of Abraham Lincoln.
When Martin Luther King Jnr was assassinated
I took my first day off in ten years.

Well, I left Memphis forty years ago,
not in a coffin, thank the Lord,
but in a Greyhound bus.

New York. Nobody handed me the keys to the city.
The day after I got off that bus
I walked in and out of fifteen restaurants,
got a job washing dishes at Taco Tony.
I still send Mr Valdez a Christmas card.

One morning I was helping
with the freshly-ironed tablecloths,
when Carmela the cashier
told me she was quitting,
intent on becoming a nurse.

She handed me a college brochure.
I enrolled the next day.

Our principal teacher, Mr Wolpe,
made tending for the anxious, the ill and the dying
sound like a privilege.
He also assured us that nursing offered fulfilment,
job security and camaraderie.

I try to remember Mr Wolpe's righteous words,
his personal belief in me—and the smell of his cologne,
when I have an especially trying day.

Frank Brookmeyer is wheeled into the ward

"Wake up, Perez!" "Frank! You made it. Long time

no see." "It is, isn't it. How're you, Filipe? You look well."

"Discharged—in a day or two, they tell me."

"Not back to work?" "No. Though no one's clear about that.

The doctors are vague and say three weeks, maybe, 'with some

physiotherapy', 'with some rest', 'with some gym work', some 'light duties'.

They're all over the shop. The force can't make its mind up—

we're *very much needed* or we 'need a rest'. They seem

to be talking about both of us. But I see you're not moving too fast.

You might take a while to get back on your feet?"

"I'll be out of here in a few weeks but embarking on

a lengthy course of rehabilitation … that it makes me tired

thinking about. So a while, yes." Brookmeyer paused.

"McFerran been around?"

"He was in a few days ago and he's coming in today." "Ask any questions?"

"He said nothing—I don't know why he came. Asked if I'd been talking

to you. Annoyed you were 'still asleep'." "Listen, when he does start,

stay vague—you don't remember anything *exactly*—when you drew your gun,

where you were precisely, what was said, the sequence of events."

"He did begin to ask something—about cavalry, the 'acting cavalry',

and looked at me as though I should help. Then he looked out

the window again, said it didn't matter it would keep.

Said you were *a fine man* and left." "Dangerous flake. How

he ever got where he did …!"

Schoolgirl

The long banks of windows disclose nothing
of what goes on inside—and Chloe Saulnier
does not actually formulate the question. Television

would inform her imagining—if the building were not clearly
much older than any program she might have watched. Must
it be more sombre, more severe than she can picture?

Chloe cannot tell—but sees a glass of water,
tall; filled; standing somewhere near a window sill—
and a window, partially open, disclosing nothing of the view.

Grey walls. There is no soundtrack to this image—
only a sense of quietness, of nothing changing, of time moving
slowly by. This is 'recovery', a long waiting for health—

as experienced by an old person—a woman probably—
though Chloe does not picture her, just her patience.
Then she sees herself, viewed from above and distant, in her school uniform,

as from these windows.

Mariette Handke talks with her book group friends

Since the heart attack
I've changed,
drive slower on the freeway,
cook proper meals,
no longer use the microwave.

At our monthly meeting
it used to be me
who hadn't read or finished the novel
we'd chosen to discuss.
Now I make notes,
sometimes read a passage out loud.

I telephoned Debra last week.
She's living in Chico, California,
with a short order cook named Raymond.
I down-played my recovery,
the sessions with the hospital psychiatrist,
didn't mention my terror at night,
imagining my father in the fold of the bedroom curtains,
the punishing belt, in his right hand.

If I've learned anything
it's to practise gratitude,
so I try to remind myself I have
a heartbeat, and a daughter,
all of Proust, Melville and Dickens to read.

SIXPACK FOUR

Theo Wong and Wayne Lech, the staff recreation room, St Vincent's Hospital, Fitzroy

I'm Chinese but it doesn't mean
I'm automatically going to thrash you
at table tennis, Wayne, but let's play—
until Henderson and Chubbs finish their game of chess.
Here, I'll take this, um, ratty-looking bat—
looks like someone's chewed on the handle.

Nice shot! See, *you're* the natural.

Hey, yesterday in the staff canteen?
when they had mushroom and tomato lasagne
on the menu?
I invited Tina from Radiology out on a date.
(Good shot!)
I was thinking of taking her
to that theatre restaurant, Dracula's,
but Chubbs suggested the Cellar Bar.
For once he's right. (You got
lucky there.)
I went past it yesterday evening.
The windows are tinted,
the seating is comfortable
and they have subdued lighting.
As you can see I've still got some acne.

For myself, I'm planning to order

the spaghetti marinara with white wine and capers,

the more sophisticated choice.

I've got to make sure I don't eat too quickly.

What? Yes, yes I am nervous.

If you've got any tips, Wayne,

I'm listening, I'll take notes.

Don't be modest, c'mon.

You dated Svetlana from Colorectal for two years.

Ah, the ball's gone under the Coke machine.

I'll fish it out.

Best out of three? It's my serve.

Interview One

"I have to ask these questions, as you will both know,

because … there is a deal of public interest—but not only public …"

"Who else is interested?" "Well, it was such a large haul

other agencies wonder how they missed it."

"Inattention?" "I can hardly put that to them, Frank.

You know that." "Well someone should." "They want to know

what was your connection." "There was no connection."

"No mention of drugs when you called it in."

"We didn't know of any." "Then what were you doing there?

You must see …" "It didn't look right. It's a street we've used

on and off for years. We park in it, we have lunch there."

"There is a suggestion you parked there

regularly." "Witness testimonies will tell you that.

We were eating." "They do, in fact, say you were eating

and taking a long time about it." "We knew that street.

It had changed, so we kept coming back to see

what it was about it. Kids play there—

balls, hoops and what have you. They own it.

But they never go near that refurbished building.

We asked. They shrugged." "Finally …" "Finally one of them

said his dad warned him *not to go near it*." "These kids were over everything."

"Everything else." "There's a suggestion—I know that both of you

have been injured—and no one takes that lightly—there is some suggestion,"

McFerran looked at them sharply—"that you

could have entered on the scene with undue—with cur,
curvilinear, without due coov-" "Are there suggestions
of lack of due care, Inspector, that we've been *cavalier,*
feckless?" "It amounts to the same thing." "Well,
'feckless' is more your 'care-free', 'who cares'. 'Cavalier', now,
is more *in-cautious*." "At all times we exercised due caution."
"Thank you, Sgt Perez—that was what I wanted to hear.
On the other hand. Two officers wounded,
one man dead, a major crime operation quickly abandoned.
No arrests made, even subsequently." "All this indicates
No Connection, sir." "Sir, we went in." "Yes, you've been
very brave." He looked away. "Well, you'll have to excuse me."

#

"Well," says Perez, "'cavalier'."
"Even now he doesn't know the word. Probably,"
says Brookmeyer. He looks up to the high, frosted windows
in the space they have been interviewed in.
Stacked chairs line the wall beneath the line of glass.
A kind of non-room.
"A little lie down?"
They make their way back to the ward.
"*You* lie down, Frank. I'm going for a walk."
Filipe watches Frank begin to change back into his pyjamas,
leaves when he is settled.

Meeting of Minds

Perez pushes out the front doors—when he finds them—
down the few steps, and out onto the street
and turns left and walks. Ten-thirty, eleven. No one about.
He is almost tempted to ask the girl, a schoolgirl,
what she is doing out and about and not in class—
but why should he? He laughs, looks up at the building
that has held him for more than two weeks.
It looks bleak, almost 'Soviet' to his imagination.
Built, he figures, some time in the seventies. Maybe earlier.
As a policeman he has known only its Emergency entrance.
This is what the larger whole looks like.

For her part, the schoolgirl—Chloe—is amused at
the small, stockily built man before her
who looks so much like her idea of a plain
clothes policeman. And she wonders if he is one. (No,
she thinks, on principle.) He is wearing a pale
mustard-yellow suit, white shirt, red tie (narrow),
has a dark moustache, a heart-shaped face—a look of impatience.
He gazes at her briefly and she feels she is 'clocked',
then discounted.

They pass each other—Chloe on to St Bridget's. Perez

walks a hundred feet—to a small, triangular park—

some trees, a round pond about a fountain—sits

and calls his wife.

Sister Fiorelli of the Daughters of Divine Zeal, Richmond

Since Sister Annunciata died,
I've been placed in charge of the hospital chapel.

Saturday afternoons I walk down Bridge Road
to see the florist, Mr Toscano.
I choose white lilies if he has them. Two bunches.
He never allows me to pay.

When I get to the chapel,
there's usually someone there,
kneeling or sitting,
sometimes clutching
a handkerchief—
usually a woman.

The fact that I'm a woman,
a somewhat dutiful example,
enables them to speak.
Of course, they are worried
about a loved one,
perhaps cruelly fated to soon slip
from this world.

Often there's self-blame,

the confession of personal flaws.

These are overworked women,

Italian, Greek, Vietnamese, Eritrean,

grappling with more than

a facility with language.

I listen, suggest,

whatever seems appropriate, achievable,

even if that's only

a taxi ride home.

The morning clientele at Pellegrini's

A trio of nurses,

their faces animated by coffee and gossip,

laugh loudly, another night shift done.

Closer to Claude and the café entrance,

sits an elderly man, pouring sugar into his black coffee.

He talks to Paul, the barista—in Italian,

interspersed with some English.

The weather. No rain.

The soccer. Another loss for the Socceroos.

Life since his Maria died. Admits to going more often

out to Flemington racecourse.

The young people on the train.

So many with tattoos. There was a time

when only sailors, jailbirds and Pacific islanders had them.

Claude sketches the clientele's faces,

studies each individual when they pause then gaze

into the café mirrors,

at their iPhone,

the bags of Vittoria coffee

which line the postcard-cluttered shelves

behind the café counter.

Nino's there, surveying the café

from the threshold of the kitchen.

He's wearing one of his signature check shirts,

a coffee-stained tea towel draped over his right shoulder.

In comes the guy from American Tailors—

Sebastian?—he'll talk to anyone with two ears—

about his love of opera, his favourite recordings,

how Mario Del Monaco

is the greatest tenor of all time.

Claude sketches. Today his lines and shadings

are sure, controlled, pleasing to his eye.

Interview Two

                    "It might have been better

if you had withdrawn at that point."

"We need never have got out of the car."

"Yes. I take your point. At this stage you had

drawn your guns and *you* had your safety catch off."

"At some time after we passed the first floor, sir.

We'd not been able to enter—but had seen

an AK40 visible through the door." "And you, Perez?"

"I had my gun out, sir—not sure when I armed it."

"And yet your gun killed the only victim." "Yes, sir.

They surprised us on the third floor."

"There was a lot more blood …" "And there are unrecovered

bullets—so you were firing at others, Brookmeyer."

"At three other men." "Of whom you know you hit one.

In fact the blood found indicates two others at least, and witnesses

indicate four drove away. Were you in your opinion

adequately… were you caville in your …? "Cavalier, sir?

Not in my judgement." "Feckless … It amounts to the same thing."

"Well, not quite—but I don't think we were either one."

"No, on balance, I'm glad you did what you did—

your instincts were right. You did well

to come out of it alive." He closes his file,

nods and is gone.

"'Cavalier'."

"Must've looked it up," says Filipe.

#

"Well, that went well. Nervous disposition, McFerran."
"Not a very American *term*, not very *New York*—'feckless'."
"Still, we learnt something." "One dead, we knew that."
"The blood of two others you must've hit, given
all the bullets they haven't recovered—I still had four
in my gun." "At least five people including the dead man,
judging by witness accounts." "Maybe more."
"McFerran seemed glad not to have to say
'cavalier' again." "Ha ha, yeah. A technical term."
"Not great to re-live, right?" "True that."
"'Now I can hardly put that to them, Frank'," says Perez,
"'*You* know that'." "'You know that'," Frank repeats and nods.
"*There was* no *connection*," Perez says. "Do you think he got that?"
"Yes—and he was relieved 'cavalier' was not going to come round again."
"Might come down to that?" "Ha ha."

SIXPACK FIVE

Reading Matter

Veronika has come down to the bottom
                                   of the hospital,
out the back—charged with bringing up some
fresh books for the television room, and
for some of the older women who particularly like to
                                                  read.

What is this woman's name, Margrethe or
                                   something like that?

But the latter knows she's coming, and merely points—
to a box on a low table. Books.
Veronika selects a dozen. There are two copies
of one, so she puts one back. "Crap, that one,"
says the woman. "In fact they're all crap."
"In fact," she says with a delighted grin, "*books* are crap,"
and laughs. Veronika nods, chooses a few.
On the way up in the lift she glances at *Gold Fools.*
It looks relatively new. Immediately it feels
like one of the most tedious and exasperating books
she has ever read. She reformulates this to herself,
casting it in the interrogative—*"Was it,"*
she says to herself, *"one of the most exasperating books
Veronika had ever read?"* and laughs. She heads to the TV room.

The Golden Carp Clinic, Umeda, Osaka

Doctor Murata's waiting room.

On the low table,

issues of *National Geographic* reveal

all the places I've never been.

I sit here, cannot quell these volleys of coughs.

Beneath my ribs

autumn leaves fall.

My Buddhist parents

were appalled when I became an actor,

but acting allows me

to leave the limitations of myself—

I don my costume, makeup,

choose from a wardrobe of accents,

and for a season become

a king, thief, murderer, sage, clown or slave.

When my parents died in the apartment fire,

I assumed my most challenging role,

the grieving son.

No critic attended the funeral,

only a single aunt

who I hadn't seen for years.

Now my role is one of patient.
I have few lines, little sleep.

Whatever Doctor Murata finds,
I'll shuffle the long way home,
try to limit my whisky to three glasses.

Sayaka Takemori, student, Chiba University

It was the first day of Spring.
I joined the line of medical students,
unusually hushed as they spiralled down the stairs
to the chilly basement.

There was some initial note-taking,
then my name was the first one called.
I looked down at the cadaver
exposed on the dissecting table.
Despite the pathologist's prompting
I couldn't bring myself
to make the first incision in the teenage boy's chest.
He reminded me of Kenji.

I rushed from the disinfected room,
up the basement stairs into natural light, fresh air.
I vomited on the university lawn.

The next morning I went to the Careers Guidance Officer.
He listened with impressive calm,
then slid four course brochures towards me.
I studied them, rejected
Architecture, Commerce and Urban Planning,
chose Horticulture.

Since making that choice
I almost skip to the University library.
Reverently I study each botanical drawing,
the intricacy of certain plants, the melody
and sometimes gravity of their Latin names.

I remember my mother more often now—
her evening ritual of tending the mini-jungle
which flourished on her apartment balcony.
How tenderly she wiped the dust
from each waxy leaf and frond.
I was pleased to see her occupied, after the divorce.

Going Home

On the bus there are only two passengers—Chloe,
having studied till 9, coming home now, late, from the library,
hungry—and the Marlene Dietrich woman, as Chloe
thinks of her—who is often on it, along with the nurses
and workers who are usually on board. The bus is silent.

The woman, who is reading a small book about 'fools',
says precisely, "Har. Har." Chloe, at the back, looks
at the woman, who turns to the dark window,
and says to her reflection, "*Did* she think, with approval,
that this was *really* 'one funny guy'?"

Aesthetics (The Cleaners)

"They'll last much longer than venetians,"

       Esther says. "They're depressing,

but they'll last a lot longer."

                "How long?"

"They'll still be here when the place dies."

                     "*Dies?*

It's brand new. How long do you think

this place will last, before they pull it down?"

                       "Thirty years."

"Thirty?" he considers, "I suppose that's right.

                    Or they might refurbish it."

"Thirty years I reckon—and they won't have cleaned them

                           either.

They don't show dirt."

             "They're awful. They take *years*

                  off your life.

It's awful to talk about vertical blinds.

Want to get a coffee?"

            They find the kind of 'coffee station'

that passes for a coffee lounge—or perhaps it doesn't—

buy coffees, and a *Picnic* for Craig. He looks at it

with a sort of affection, its bright red, bright yellow,

the optimism of the wrapper's jagged design.

Esther watches a bird—a sparrow, that is trapped inside—

hop along against the glass searching for food.
Craig watches it too. It flies away, comes back,

                                            flutters away again.

"What next?" he asks Esther. They stand.

Kenji Izumi talks to his friend
Shiraha Okamoto

Sayaka's dropped out of Medicine
switched to Horticulture.
I miss her but she needs this time
away from her parents,
so she can breathe.

I hope Sayaka does
visit the Student Union building,
perhaps joins the chess club.
I taught her some sturdy attacks
and defences.

In daily walks around the port
and near Kema Lock,
I've been writing urban haiku—
the brutish drama of
shipping containers, cranes,
scrapyards, oil tankers—
metaphors for ingenuity, salvage and disrepair.

Are they any good?

I may write longer poems,

partly autobiographical,

about Sayaka and me,

our rudderless navigation

away from known shores,

the elongated shadows which parents cast.

SIXPACK SIX

Minoru Maki interviewed in the band room of Namba Bears, Osaka

Having a total of eight fingers
has made me
a different kind of piano player and composer.

I go for depth not speed—
to plunge the listener into a world
deeper than their glass of beer.

A recent composition, "Wake Up Dead",
is part of the soundtrack to a movie
in which I prise open the lid of a dumpster
to see who squirms there—
Beethoven in a pinstripe suit,
dislodging orange peel
from his trouser cuffs.

I'm a very light sleeper.
The sound of the family dog's toenails
on the hallway floorboards
is there in the first movement
of my jazz symphony.

My music is a homage to Osaka—

the thud of a can of Coke,

released from the clutches

of a vending machine,

the tap tap of a woman's fingernail

on the convenience store counter

as she waits for her change,

the clink of an empty sake bottle,

troubled by the wind.

The Problem of Other Minds

Reg is remembering a dog he used to have
and how he loved it. He sees her sitting before him
looking up to his face. Of course, *Can it really be love,*
he considers. A less complex affair than with
a human.

                          He would talk to Dot often,
about exactly these things—as she looked at him,
or as they walked along—amusing himself at the irony,
irritating her possibly, with the smugness of his assumptions.
"If you could talk, and started giving me advice," he says,
to her upturned face, her patient eyes, "we'd probably fall out.
Who wants another person telling you what to do?" "Make
your mind up," is that what she might say,
or would she nod?—they had dealt with this before.
Maybe only implicitly. He says to the dog—in his mind—
the dog to whom he had said things like this so many times
when they had been together, walking, passing time, "I'm
                          going to sing for you, now,
… [pause] a medley … of Sam Cooke songs" and
in his mind he casts about for which, which to start—
and mentally (in his mind) begins—
          discounts 'Sad Mood' as too sad—
begins, "We're having a party / Everybody's swinging"
but doesn't sing it, sings instead, in his mind—*back then*

as he imagines it—and without introduction, "Downhearted …
do-doot dooo—broken dreams and never really started."

"How you going there, Mr Summers." "Oh, hullo Deidre."
It is the nurse's aide. "I've come to do your toenails,
that okay? Need doing?" she asks. "No, no," he says.
"I was just thinking about an old friend." "An old girlfriend?"
"No, well yes, in a way."

In the Navy, in the Navy

Jason is at the opposite end of the infirmary
from the other occupied bunks. Flu and pneumonia,
some stomach complaints. This part of the ship
is quiet and peaceful—just the slight shudder of the engines
and the sense as of skimming across the sea.
He will be paid out, discharged—or given
land duties—which might be an idea. A land-based
sailor.

He is happy now, Jason realizes, with his injury, where,
healthy, he had not been before. He will leave the navy
with a discharge, some money, some skills. At the least,
be redeployed on shore. 'Navy'—but not a sailor.
A few more years, then out. Out immediately,
if he is not posted to a city, he thinks.

Did Mick do it—not intentionally—or did Jason
do it himself? Neither of them careful in a reliable way—
Jason's mood one of irritation that masked
despair at the navy life. Reckless. A drum had shifted,
and rolled, and crushed his hand and forearm—
which would mend.
There might be something more, to follow, from the spill
and his contact with it. No symptoms yet. He felt okay. He might need
to fake those symptoms if they didn't show—although, another thing,

you might not want to be treated for something weird like that

if you could avoid it. He would have to do some research

between here and Melbourne. A small regional hospital

might be best. Maitland, Newcastle. Suddenly there were prospects,

away from these people.

Forward planning

The bathroom scales confirm
that Sayaka had lost weight
and she's pleased with her look,
the new short haircut
and the floral-patterned sweatpants.

Three more days until Kenji visits.
Sayaka knows he'll like the Blue Note poster,
framed and hanging in the hallway,
of John Coltrane looking pensive,
perhaps listening to a playback
of "I'm Old Fashioned".

Sayaka's record collection is filed in alphabetical order,
from The Avalanches' *Since I Left You*
through to Zappa's *Lumpy Gravy*.
Kenji is bound to check.

Her trump card though
is in having found Chiba's only jazz bar, Plum Dog.
Sayaka is confident that Kenji
will like the current local band,
booked for a month-long residency—
The Walking Flowers.

Their leader, Moses Leaf,

plays a shakuhachi flute,

which he's electrified somehow.

The drummer, who goes by the name Hub Cap,

has this arsenal of homemade percussion instruments—

old pickle jars filled with different coloured buttons

which he shakes during the Latin-flavoured numbers

and an empty fish bowl which he delicately taps

with a pair of aluminium shoe horns

during some of the ballads.

Sayaka hopes that her new look, the apartment,

her choice record collection,

the existence of Plum Dog and The Walking Flowers

and, if necessary, her tears,

will sway Kenji into moving to Chiba.

Sayaka wants to have children with Kenji

If the first one's a boy

she's fine about calling him

Miles or Thelonious—

that should sweeten the deal.

Portrait of Kenji Izumi in his apartment, March 2019

I light a Seven Stars,

stand out on the balcony,

look up at the night sky.

I'm bummed that Pluto

got kicked out of the solar system,

demoted to dwarf star,

despite having a posse of five moons.

Some nights, after a few beers,

I imagine Pluto

orbiting more slowly now,

delivering Marlon Brando's classic line,

"I could have been a contender"

to passing asteroids.

I used to like reality and having a girlfriend.

Now I lie on my bed, a stale pretzel of a man,

listen to Saint Etienne's version of

"Only Love Can Break Your Heart"—

then I rise to play it again.

Selling Yourself

"Balthus, Chagall, Jane Freilicher," he says,

and the critic writes it down. "But there also has to be

will—you must take control, the intelligence

assert itself. Certain English, certain Germans,"

he says, wondering who, Bellmer?

John Virtue? Then, with great seriousness, "If Brack had been

greater ..." and—swiftly mysterious and final, as if

saying more—"Howard Arkley, in a few of his paintings, is our

Cezanne."

"Our Picabia?" he pretends to mishear the pen-pusher,

"We've never had one." He turns, looks bitterly across

the sea of intervening bodies, heads and faces, talking, nodding, quaffing,

to the window, as if it offered escape, as if he would rather be elsewhere

(actually, he *would* rather be), as if he can no longer bear the hubbub.

Is this too much?

But the gallery owner informs him—*and*—probably it is deliberate—

the critic—that important collectors are buying.

He hands his glass to the gallerist with a show of

distraction and decision and drifts with Lewis

outside to the balcony and they stand together facing the darkness.

"Let's give this twenty minutes, look at the stars for a while

then disappear. I think I've done it."

SIXPACK SEVEN

"That's okay, we *have* no car."

"Your husband was in the line of fire, I think—

Mrs 'Brookmeyer', is it?" "That's me. I mean,

I'm his … but I use my own name, Meyer."

"German name." "Yes. Yes, it is." "Not as German

                                        as me,"

the woman smiled as she looked at Frank's file.

She looked up, and down again for the name—"Hello

… *Helen*," she read from the notes.

"Veronika," she offered. Their eyes met. She said,

"Your husband's *partner* will be out of here any day now,

I should imagine." "And Frank?" "Frank lost a good deal

                                        more blood

and had more extensive wounds, though none so close to a major organ.

Mr Perez could have been gone. Your husband

will have to be determined and *patient*

to recover full mobility. The leg will be okay. The arm

will take time." "Frank's patient enough," says Helen. "Determined, I don't know.

He can be." "It will be worth it. Will he retire?" Veronika asked.

"Even retired," she said, "it is good to have two arms I think, arms that

function properly." "Yes. Frank will see it that way." "I don't think

he will retire," Helen said, as the therapist replaced the file, then

changed her mind, handed it to her. Closed. Helen opened it.

"A lot of movement over the first few weeks," Veronika went on.

"He *must* retire, for a little while, and go on holiday.

He must not, now, sit.

He has mended, you understand, but some things must be trained,

to work as before.

I will suggest that he gets leave. An easy walking tour

would be good, but Americans—*what to do with the car?*" she smiled.

Claude Hartigan attends his second solo exhibition, Tacit Galleries, Collingwood

Wow, the gallery's crowded.

I need to sell some paintings.

Winter is coming. I'd like to buy a couple of tonnes

of firewood for the studio fireplace

and some new records, not that I'm tired of Coltrane.

That guy, with the reddish tinge in his hair,

taking a second look at *Girl Reading by the Yarra,*

I've seen his face somewhere. Oh yeah,

a black and white author photo in *Art Monthly*.

He's that art critic. MacVicar or McIver—

quite knowledgeable. Even able to put some humour

in a review. Tactful if he broaches the subject

of an artist's decline.

He hasn't zeroed in on the refreshments table—

a good sign. Oh-oh—he's taken out his notepad,

is writing. The guy uses a fountain pen.

I'm going to relax now, shake a few necessary hands,

kiss a few Brighton and Toorak cheeks.

Mustn't drink too much. That's what killed Lester Young,

old Mr. Crumpled Suit.

The art critic looks like a jazzhead.

Maybe I'll talk to him,

not as a career move, a rubbing shoulders thing—

more a case of two roosters acknowledging each other

in the big barnyard of Australian art.

Band video shoot

Bob has blu-tacked a handmade sign
to the back of his Roland Jupiter—
"This Machine Kills Lawyers".

Here comes Paul The Tailor with the gold suits
for the boys to wear. The trouser legs are too long
but make a kind of anti-fashion statement.
Put your scissors away, Paul. Get yourself a drink.

Megan looks gorgeous— the long bob haircut,
her ski jump nose, the daisy-patterned pullover—Oxfam chic.
Clyde, make sure you have
a long enough lead for the wind machine.

Sarah, please have another honey and lemon drink.
Gargle some salt and water. If you're still sniffling
and sneezing when we're ready, Megan will do the vocal on
"Only Love Will Break Your Heart".

Don't sulk. Sit over in that chair. Paul looks lonely.
C'mon, go over and talk to him. He likes you.

A Favour

"Marketable, I should have thought," said the artist, driving.
Beside him, stolid, silent, sat Lewis in his usual
linen jacket, rumpled but impeccable shirt, Levi's, loafers.
The gallery director, who had asked the question, was emboldened:
"I'm considering adding him to our list."
There was silence. "Is he really one of ours?" he continued,
as if wondering aloud. Lewis regarded his phone.
"I doubt we are so very alike," the artist said, "Any of us.

Hartigan is not, so far, much collected," he went on—"which
    in one sense means
there are *sales to make.*   And there is a sudden interest in him, in
his subject matter, in Claude himself." "Yes. From the wrong side
of the tracks—there's *that* frisson." "I don't think he is, you'll find.
I think at some time he 'moved' there—and would probably like to move
    back."
Some streetlights are out as they cross Merri Creek.
"The art itself," Lewis surprises them—but does not finish the sentence.
A moment passes.

"Think *Egon Schiele, Elizabeth Peyton, Bill Henson* ...
is the usual opinion. His drawing is not at base decorative,
or stylized. It hews to observation and there is its strength.
The decorative and emotional payout comes from his quickness,
his sharpness," says the artist. "He *spares* detail—he also hunts it."

"Quite," says the gallerist, and adds, after a moment, "Well put."
He will give Claude a show. "I wouldn't say I'd be keen
to know him," a final touch.   Even so, the gallerist's mind
is made up.

A Withdrawal (Darwin)

The children were fanned out in an arc before the TV—
their mother Brenda Hall, beyond one small curly head,
was immediately on her right, hubby Jim Hall just beyond Brenda.
The room laughed admiringly at *Peppa Pig*—as did
her own daughter, but not so much. The friendly neighbours—
whom she was glad of. Still, something about it
got her down. What was it they liked so particularly—
Peppa's English vowels and complacency? Was the language
innocent? More innocent than their own, and its lies,
the reality it masked? English English told *different* lies,
she supposed, different than Australian? Perhaps
all nations lied? Except her own.
But they had never become a nation.
Perhaps they would and had better start lying—
perhaps they had begun already? No. They hadn't.
She tried for seconds to tamp these thoughts down.
Here she was, living with Whitey. The Halls were nice—
and nice to her, to Yvonne, head turned to her now, enquiringly,
silhouetted against the screen—dependent though, all of it,
she was sure, on her middle class bona fides—income,
rent, *education.* Hers might be superior to theirs—
lending parity (a degree of it, grounds for it) with their white skin.
It could be withdrawn. Friends.

Portrait of Derek Cosmo, manager

When there are two songwriters in a band,
you've got an ego situation—
soothing one, praising the other, but not overly.
And not overtly.
I remind them of their
first winter of pop discontent—
a flea-pit share house in Willesden,
huddled around the heater and the stereo,
listening to The Smiths.

Ideas are good, encouraged, but I have this vision,
so when Bob started talking about
hauling in a Mellotron to the studio,
I had to placate him, a little steering.
In the end he was happy to hire a theremin.
It's there on the forthcoming album.

I place great value on our weekly band meetings,
to address any deviation from what I see
as the collective image.
There has been heated debate over the boys
continuing to wear the gold suits.
Sarah's on side, championing my suggested move
to industrial garb. I see the next video being shot
in an auto assembly plant, a fitting homage
to the band's love of the Motor City Sound.

Influences are fine, but not imitation.
As gently as possible I tell Bob
he's not Brian Wilson,
this is London not Santa Monica,
to forget about mentioning surf
in any of his songs.

SIXPACK EIGHT

Derek Cosmo talks about Ian

Ian's the quiet one in the band,
a multi-instrumentalist.
It was his idea, those sampled harpsichord trills
on the first single.

He's serious, wound up tight,
doesn't smoke or drink coffee,
won't be part of interviews.
Anything besides the music,
he considers pollution.

When Ian read about Leonard Cohen
spending seven years in a Californian monastery
I was worried, but then I played Ian some 45's,
including one by an Australian group, The Sunnyboys,
their single "Alone With You".
Ian loved the jingle jangle guitars, the backing vocals,
the meat and potatoes drumming—
the flash, the pace of that 45 and we were back on track.

As a manager, you won't find me

bare-chested in a hammock on Hydra

while the band slogs their way through a world tour.

I'm there at every gig, work the merchandise table,

make sure there's mineral water in the dressing-room,

tell each photographer to not use the flash

when taking pictures of him, Ian.

He's almost too sensitive for this life,

why his songs are so good.

Open Plan Kitchen, Deck

"Stay for a glass of something?" Neville prompted.

She was torn, "Oh, I *would*." "Got to get Yvonne?" Amanda guessed.

"Yes," said Kate—"though I'd rather be here."

She said, "I'll get Dave to get her." "They won't mind will they?"

"They can't," she answered Amanda, "Dave will do just as well."

She phoned her husband. "Says yeah, but he wants to be at home,"

she reported, "So just the one."

                                "What are they like anyway,

Brenda and Jim?" "They're okay. Hard to know what they think—

or whether they try not to a lot of the time. There's

never much said,

                    and I get the feeling I've been handed a script—

of things you can talk about: and there's *not much on the list*.

A lot of stuff would be out of bounds.

                             They'd be very nervous

if I brought up refugees, or …"   "Race."

                                  "Yeah. Well.

I don't know if they talk about it themselves."

"Even class," she added.

                        "Dangerous topic."

"People don't like to feel guilt."

                            "It'd be as if I'd

turned some tables on them …"

"*J'accuse',*" said Nev.

"Yeah," she agreed.

"But nice *enough,* not awful. You can *be* there, though, and think,
This is Australia—and not feel like you're part of it."

"What—you're not an Australian?"

"Well, maybe No.
Not by invitation."

"Maybe they *are* inviting you.
Their kids play with Yvonne?"

"Oh yes, they're her friends sure enough.
Though not like with you, Elly." Elly looked up, a small figure
across the room. "Where's Vonnie, Aunty Kate?"
"The Sullivans'," said Kate as a joke, and corrected it,
"The Halls'."

"So you're not an Australian then."

"Well, when we
take the place back we can change the name.
Pearson's probably got something picked."
"Ha ha." "The Halls can stay.

(Better get over there.)"
Kate waved. "Goodnight, Aunty Kate," called Elly. She left.

Moths were hovering in a distant cloud across the road
about the porch light of the Halls' place, a pool of green
beneath.

Dolphy and Goethe

Plastic bunting snapped and thrummed in the wind
the loneliest, the saddest, the cruellest sound,
pointless and punitive and empty—a denial
of all promise. Nothing good would happen while
the wind blew and the sun's weak light shone down.

Claire passed her hand for warmth under
Mark's jumper, held the flesh of his side. They swayed
together, wasted. At last the dealer's car arrived,
slowed and the window wound down. He beckoned, smiled
and they moved towards him climbed in gave him what they'd been paid

for what they'd sold. Vince counted out some notes
and supplied the bags they'd sell tonight their own share included,
dropped them near the hospital, A&E. They went in, shot up
marched home and slept the sleep of the just, woke, cut
the deals for that night, ate, showered. The muted

sound of Mark whistling, whistling '2 4 5'—that he did
when he was happy—made her smile. She cleaned her teeth
applied eye-liner, hummed herself. She began to read
Iphigenia in Tauris, made tea in a pot, spread butter on bread.

Karl Broadfoot remembers

Nadua would come into the general store,
after selling a mess of bracelets and necklaces
at a county fair, offer no greeting, no weather talk.
Words were coins she wanted to keep.
At most I'd get—"Pinto beans. Twelve cans."
A pause, a rub of her chin, then
"Tobacco. Matches. Six candles."

Then the goodbye of her back
with that long braid of black hair.
The shuffle of her moccasins
out the spring-hinged door.

Nadua cooked, smoked her pipe,
did her thinking, down by the Little Wichita River,
where she slept in a wind-threatened teepee.

One Sunday morning
my bicycle directed me away from Sunday school,
to Nadua's camp.
She heard me yelp when her legion of chickens
pecked at my ankles, drew blood.

Nadua led me to the river,
swabbed at the wound with my bandana
which she'd loosened from my neck.

Having passed the chicken initiation,
Nadua and me sat on the riverbank.
She proceeded to point
at a boulder, a tuft of river grass,
a buzzard perched on the a dead tree,
repeated the name for each in Comanche,

became my Sunday school.
I learned how to trap polecats and jackrabbits,
how to skin them and cure their pelts.

By the time the U.S. entered the war,
I was 18 and enlisted.
When I told Nadua,
she spat on the ground,
ran to her teepee,
emerged with a necklace
made of river stones and braided leather,
hung it round my neck.

I looked at Nadua, once more
withholding her words, who knew that words
should never be squandered on a fool—
and I kicked the dirt with my boot tip,
cursed the war in myself.

Derek Cosmo reports

The break from London has been good for Ian—
being back at his Mum's,
fed her sturdy home-cooking.

Studio time's been booked for July.
Can't let the band's momentum slow too much.
There's a small but growing fanbase in France,
partly due to Sarah's look in the last video—
her hoop earrings and pout.

I flew to Wicklow again last week.
Fascinating to see
Ian's largely unchanged teenage bedroom,
the poster of Marc Bolan,
on the dresser, a dusty Rubik's Cube.

Ian's been listening to the Special AKA album,
In the Studio. The layers, the mosaic of sound,
the cross-pollination—
Cuba meets Jamaica via Coventry.
Trumpet. Trombone. Melodica. Cow Bells.
Commentary on the
hurt and hateful, the
empty wallet and pint glass.

He's learning that songs can take months
to finesse—the sifting, the mix.

And with him I often have to
shift from sympathetic to firm.
Fatherly—but not cloying.

Heavy-handed is out.

Marta Saulnier

Marta Saulnier looks down, from a seventh floor balcony,
on elm trees and between them to the street and the broad sidewalks
that run either side: the long parade-like view
the hospital creates, stepped as it is, well back from the hue
and cry—the energy—of the street—the postcard-like sorts

of view that bring to mind the phrase *Champs-Élysées*.
No *Arc de Triomphe* at the further end—
but the pedestrians walk here with more space around them, an air
of elegance, Cartesian calm, of, almost, *Last Year
At Marienbad*. She sees her daughter's charming blend

of thoughtful schoolgirl and young adult poise—
that she will see soon now literally when Chloe will appear,
her upright posture, the broad hat and St Bridget's blue
uniform. She waters the plants, puts two plates, two
cups and their saucers out on the white iron table. Here

she will sit with Chloe and they will discuss their day,
have coffee and cake, or fruit. Later, a small meal,
before they will go out together to *Cul de Sac* or *Duck Soup*
or *Horse Feathers*, at their currently preferred small cinema. A burly man
     in a yellow suit,
had been about to accost Chloe this morning, then thought better of it. She'll

remind her: he had turned abruptly

and gone into the hospital. Chloe knows her mother's gaze

follows her for some moments each morning—but from such a height

it feels no invasion of privacy or *too much love:* like

the gaze with which she herself picks out Marta some days

thread her way between others, cross the park, to the library:

dusk, her mother's tailored grey suit and sometimes, even,

pill box hat that Chloe loves. "'The heroism'," Chloe thinks,

"'of modern day life'," its myriad stories—and of hers—which she thinks

will follow her mother's: law, librarianship, medicine?

SIXPACK NINE

Filipe Calls On Frank

"*Two* pieces of good news, Filipe."

Filipe, in the empty room, visiting,

is flipping through a baseball magazine, catching up

on what's happened in the game since he left.

(Hospital has seen his most intense immersion in it—

those weeks in bed. Already the game

seems more urgent now he's less engaged with it—

fugitive details—with which he can't keep pace.)

"Frank," he says, looking up. Frank Brookmeyer, on

his feet, with no frame or stick or even a look of

'balancing', stands before him. "*Two* pieces—

that can't be good luck, surely?" He crosses himself

piously, miming superstition, "Can it?"

"Not only have we moved up a number of grades—"

"Yes—I congratulate you, senior detective." "Likewise,"

says Frank. "On top of that I hear this morning—

confirming what I'd heard confidentially—

we have an assignment overseas." "A junket?"

"Yes, and we're being *cited* for bravery and initiative."

"McFerran," says Filipe.

"Exactly. He's figured the best defence to be offence—so he's

recommended us." Frank paused, he looked down at Filipe's table—

the magazines, the sports pages—"How are the Giants doing?"

"Who cares?" says Filipe, he stretches and stands, slaps Frank

solicitously on the shoulder. "How are *you?*" "Fine," says Frank—
"Better than James Brown. Helen and I are off on a trip through
Maine, New England—a 'walking tour'—prescribed by the physio."
"The German woman—Marlene?" "Veronika." "Yeah, that's right."

"I get back on the 6th—August—she'll reassess, and I'll be
back on duty." "Which consists?" "Of preparing for a trip."
"Oh yeah. Where we going?" "Down Under—Australia!"
"Do we want to go there?" "We do. Sun, beaches, wildlife."
"Wildlife? What have they got?" "We're going to Sydney.
I doubt we'll see even a kangaroo. We wait for their system
to process some guy and we bring him back for trial.
White collar crime." "The best. Well that's great.
I'll tell the wife," says Filipe. "Been advised 'three weeks' is the estimate,
and McFerran feels we should 'not hurry back', I gather."
"What are we going to do there?" "Get a tan—I'm going to be walking
the long beach of Coogee twice a day, if you care to join me."
"I will. Is Helen coming?" "She is." "I'll talk to Estelle.
Wow, Australia. Other side of the world isn't it?" "Yep."
"'Yippee'," says Filipe, guardedly. "Nice place, so I hear," says Frank.

Ian imagines an interview with
John Peel for the BBC

Unless on tour, I take a long morning walk,
past on-going construction along the Thames.
There's never been a signature skyline—
the belief in one is there though, when you listen
to 'Waterloo Sunset'.

Derek keeps telling the band that music's a marketplace,
encourages us to
listen to the competition, raise the stakes,
'remember the dancefloor'.

Living alone, as you'll appreciate, I can indulge myself,
play Moondog, King Pleasure, early Donovan.
Derek's infuriated that sometimes
I don't answer the phone, respond to text messages.

There's only me to stop me
writing a symphony about a motorway
or the humpback whale.

I circle words in jumble sale books.
A phrase may seed a song.

I've been called melancholic, but I've got the strength
to tear off that label now.

I'm off medication. Early days.
I spend quite a lot of time, hours,
out on the balcony.

The sound of trains
slowing for Charing Cross Station,
I may be able to turn into a riff.

Music mad

Sarah looks out the train window.
There's a disused gasometer,
backyard wooden fences slouching,
graffiti emblazoned at defiant heights
on railway bridges,
the brickwork of former knitting mills.

London. Where the exhausted and exulted live,
sometimes sobered or halted by a heart attack—
for example, her neurosurgeon father. Such a busy man—
as if that's applaudable, the correct use of days.

There are tensions in the band. Bob wants
more emphasis on the lyrics, to place them
in the forefront of each mix.
Ian is adamant that instrumentals feature—
the album, a soundtrack for the restless,
shoplifting, vandalising for the adrenalin rush, the lark,
drifting stoned or pilled through the streets
of Camden, Kentish Town, a playlist world.

Sarah remembers auditioning,
how Derek noticed her scuffed shoes,
the button missing on her suede jacket,
but she knew the right distance to stand from the mic,

held the lyric sheet steady,

sensed which words needed to float or pierce.

Her own lyrics, a solo album one day—

Sarah allows herself these aspirations

as she enters Mario's Café,

navigates past tables and chairs

to where Derek is seated,

and after ordering a pot of tea and a cinnamon bun,

they begin to talk about Bob and Ian,

who have known each other

since high school.

Gold Fools

"Ronnie?" "Ah, Frank! Come in. Your leg
is alright, I think? Every time I look out the window
I see you walking up and down. Does your leg feel better?"
"It feels the same, but I think I am going further each day."
"Good." "So it's getting stronger." "It is gaining strength, yes.
I want you also to use the steps in the park—stairs anywhere—
but the park is best if you need to sit down and rest."

"I'm on to it. Listen, Veronika, have you got anything I can read?
I'm going out of my mind." "Not much." "What about this?"
Frank picks up a small book from the pile. "Veird,"
says Veronika. "What's it about? These don't look much good,"
Frank casts a glance over the other titles. "Cowboys," says Veronika,
"a parody." "Cowboys," says Brookmeyer, "Why bother?" "Try it, Frank,"
says Veronika. She watches Frank stand carefully. "Might
have to do," says Frank. "I leave soon," he says.
"I'll see you for your assessment when you get back."

"Frank!" "What?" "Pass on my regards to your wife."

A Parting Of Ways

"They also gave us this," says Martin, wheeling in

a tea urn on a trolley. He lifts it and places it

before Betty. "Who did, Martin?" "Scout Hall," he says.

"Oh, this is much more useful." She considers it.

"We might almost keep it for ourselves," she says.

"Can we? Is it in our charter?" Martin wonders.

"Well who's going to check?" asks Betty.

"You don't look well, Martin," she examines him.

He would usually pursue his point, his objection—

though why was always the question, *why* would he?

Not today evidently.

"Big night," he said. He seemed to reel at the memory.

"Oh?" she said. "Quiz night," he elaborates. "Oh, yes—

with Margie, isn't it?" Martin is silent. A falling out.

Mr Atherton, on a morphine drip, Bed 5

Nurse or niece?

nausea

the cause of your

collapse

relapse

blood in your …

monitoring the level

the devil

all the kings …

do all the kings mend?

Faint pulse

laboured breathing

little purpose, these further tests …

Father is here now, to bless

please notify his king …

his relatives, nurse

say he was pleasant to the staff

help me now

draw those curtains.

SIXPACK TEN

The hour before dawn

The car crash. The funeral.
Claire avoids Kentish Town now,
that roundabout.

There wasn't an autopsy.
Religious reasons.

Claire can't bring herself to
delete the photos of her and Sylvie
in São Paulo.

Tomorrow she'll email Aloysio,
the DJ who'd befriended them,
wasn't predatory.

People talk about hindsight, foresight.
Claire had believed in spontaneity.
The joyride. The dare.

Regret. Claire had thought that
was for older people.

Some Roaches

for Dave Edmunds

"Well-o well-o Wop, Wep Wep-wep.
Well-o Wello Wop." At some point in this refrain
I hear the screen door slam and Janet or whatever her name is
next door come down the wooden steps. "Hey!" she calls out.
"Hey, are you there Arnold, neighbour?"
"Yes," I say. (What's this about?) "Why?" "A proposition,"
says Jane. "I've cooked early and I'm going out." "Right,"
I say. "The thing is," says Jane, "It's going to smell pretty bad
for quite a few hours—in my place, and yours as well probably.
I'm getting my apartment fumigated." "Oh."
"You should close all your windows." "Right."
"I should have warned you. Anyway, I've cooked lots,
so if you haven't other plans eat with me. We could go out.
Get a drink maybe. Is that alright?" "Sure. No plans. Nice!"
"Half an hour."

Tonight's The Night

Open, plan kitchen, deck the manager when he
walks through the door. Empty the till, wipe the
                             bookings on the computer—
ha ha, that will cause some fun when they start rocking up
take the van and all the spare keys as they're hanging there too
and drive out of town. My old car is down the coast—
a 'bach' in my New Zealand friends' view—take it, leave the van
and make for Fremantle. Jump a ship right there.
Turn up in Christchurch and sail to New Caledonia,
where I start as a chef for my old friend, Dave.
Dave Holden. But under another name—
Waldo de Planck. Oh-oh, here he comes now. Flatten him?
Another day. I put the money in the till—not quite
properly sorted—will he notice? and get to work—
the kitchen is laid out in exemplary fashion—something
I know he loves. I nod, keep things moving.

Poem to a paramedic

Old men and women
fall from stepladders,
while reaching for canned peaches
stored high in the pantry.

How easily they break their crockery hips.

In the ambulance
they tell you
the day started poorly—
misplaced spectacles,
couldn't find the TV remote,
missed the morning sermon
of their favourite on-screen evangelist.

There's no one to talk to
since the cat died.

The brighter ones notice that
you don't sport a wedding ring.
Some ask,
most don't.
Prying is what
their next-door neighbour does—
binoculars dangle
from his scrawny neck.

They're glad you've got this job
where you're bound to meet a lot of people.

Some days you laugh,
some days you tell them to hush
while you check
their blood pressure again.

H.A. Hayes, ward doctor, St Vincent's Hospital, 26 March 2019

Some nights I come home so tired.
Patients' woes. Their runs of bad luck.

For many it's their first time in hospital.
Some feel ashamed of this,
that they are in danger
of being a burden.

Hope—I can't write a script for it.
What I try to provide is comfort.
I listen with more than my stethoscope,
don't let the patient see me glance at my wristwatch.

Modern surgery is procedural, far less invasive
than when I started as an intern—
I tell patients this,
watch to see
if they understand,
grip their blanket less.

Some ask me to pray for them.
I nod my head.

A senior nurse calls my name.
I'm wanted elsewhere.
There's always an elsewhere
and I walk towards it
past the odd vacated bed.

Ivan

It was a disappointment. But he had to accept it and did.
Soon, as he walked home, he was aware
of a new sadness within himself. Hope, he felt,
had discarded a childish form forever. Would it be back—
diminished, but enough?
When he entered his room the brown shutters of his window
were wide open and a small wind was bringing the smell
of frying fat into the room. He went over to the window
and looked down into the alleyway which separated the Hôtel
des Ambassadeurs from a group of shacks.

There was an old lady seated in a chair in the alleyway
eating her dinner.

"Eat every bit of it!" Mr Rabinovitch said. The old lady
looked up dreamily, but she did not answer.

Mr Rabinovitch put his hand over his heart. "Le
bonheur," he whispered, "*le bonheur* ... what an angel a
happy moment is—and how nice not to have to struggle
too much for inner peace!" But you had.

ENVOI

Linda, Collingwood, Melbourne

Linda looks at her son's note: "To Mum." — *Gone to friends, have cleaned up*
you will see, back in time for dinner. ("Which friend?" she thinks.)
Could we have (hint hint) lasagna, or sausages?
homework after dinner—there's almost none: Mrs Dimitryk was
away today, sick.

She puts her string bag down, eases off her shoes, laughs,
puts coffee on, has a word with their parrot as she
looks out the french doors of her apartment, past the long
chain-of-hearts plant hanging near—to a view there is no
need to see any clearer: a 'view' of car park and kids—

boys mostly—moving a ball about, or skateboarding, an elm tree
filling one side of the scene, unless she moves—to take in
the cleared land beside—waiting now, a year, to be rebuilt or
returned to the neighbourhood, as playground, or neutral space.
She nudges her discarded shoes, sensible like a nurse's,

into what counts as tidily squared away,
by the bookshelf near the door, beneath the plant—
by those same french doors, in fact.
She lowers the coffee cup, gets down on all fours
and does a stretch, or three, or four, arching and lowering her back

then sits and sips.

Jack, a pilot, gets back Friday and will be around

till Tuesday or Wednesday—so she might shop, later, tonight—or

tomorrow, is more likely.

Seated, she thinks of the view—a small portion of it

near the open field—sees it 'as from close to' (a pedestrian's view

that her current route to work does not take her past—will it

still be there when next she passes?)—two companionable armchairs

either side of a baby's car seat—baby, sat out there

with them—to nod to passersby, sip tea, ears

blasted as the traffic rolls by? What *did* happen—

it is years since anyone sat there—to judge by

the dust that greys the red vinyl underneath,

mottled by raindrops? She cannot picture, she realises, the adults

who sat there, let alone the baby: she remembers a cup,

small and plastic, faded and pink, on the landing beside them.

Anya

Andrei picked up a thin cushion on his way through
took it outside into the small yard that extended from the kitchen,
sat on the bench, his back briefly leant against the wall,
then sat forward, put his beer on the cement near his foot
and sighed a first sigh of relaxation. His eye took in what there
was to see—a tree in the corner, some shrubs, hose piled
carefully but casually in the corner. There was not a lot to see
but there was detail of course, cracks, leaves, weed,
the leaning confusion of rake, spade, some brooms;
the watering can; the hanging basket that held flowers—
and on which birds perched, stayed, or fluttered away, returned;
an area of discolouration in the concrete.

When his wife was here there had been more marked change
from day to day—the movement of objects determined by her gardening
and other activities. They did not bear looking at, in fact
they displaced him from the tiny space. Her absence returned it to him.
Now change was incremental, a matter of seasons, and was readable:
it said, you are alone and there is time and there are the seasons and there are
truths—and things age and alter and you with them.

Inside, his son Nikolai, twenty, studied. A medical student.
Each painfully conscious of the gap between them, and of
a degree of loyalty, and of increasing separation.

Note

The poem 'Ivan' is more or less a 'found' piece—lifted, with adjustments (and names changed), from the novel *Two Serious Ladies* by Jane Bowles.

THE ELSEWHERE VARIATIONS
Peter Bakowski and Ken Bolton

Born of the poetry wars of inner Melbourne

An explosive story—of twisted
mentalities and lost souls

'Irresistible. Compelling'—Millie Dickens

an arc of fugitive players cast across
Australia and the capitals of Europe,
the US, Asia

The Elsewhere Variations is a series of poems by Peter Bakowski and Ken Bolton in which themes develop, are abandoned, resurface, where poems answer, continue or oppose each other. The usual thrills of collaborative projects. But these are unusual and will get attention just on that basis—and they are variously funny, mysterious, and occasionally moving.

There are eight sets of six: forty-eight poems. They begin with a lightly fictionalised account of the poetry wars of inner Melbourne—but from there they undertake a survey of human happiness, ambition and acceptance.

For more information visit www.wakefieldpress.com.au

Wakefield Press is an independent publishing and
distribution company based in Adelaide, South Australia.
We love good stories and publish beautiful books.
To see our full range of books, please visit our website at
www.wakefieldpress.com.au
where all titles are available for purchase.
To keep up with our latest releases, news and events,
subscribe to our monthly newsletter.

Find us!

Facebook: www.facebook.com/wakefield.press
Twitter: www.twitter.com/wakefieldpress
Instagram: www.instagram.com/wakefieldpress